Ter
about Baking

ex libris

Candlestick Press

Published by:
Candlestick Press,
Diversity House, 72 Nottingham Road, Arnold, Nottingham NG5 6LF
www.candlestickpress.co.uk

Design and typesetting by Craig Twigg

Printed by Ratcliff & Roper Print Group, Nottinghamshire, UK

Selection and Introduction © Helena Nelson, 2020

Cover illustration © Alice Pattullo, 2020
www.alicepattullo.com

Candlestick Press monogram © Barbara Shaw, 2008

© Candlestick Press, 2020

ISBN 978 1 907598 80 7

Acknowledgements:

The poems in this pamphlet are reprinted from the following books, all by permission of the publishers listed unless stated otherwise. Every effort has been made to trace the copyright holders of the poems published in this book. The editor and publisher apologise if any material has been included without permission or without the appropriate acknowledgement, and would be glad to be told of anyone who has not been consulted.

Thanks are due to all the copyright holders cited below for their kind permission:

Harry Clifton, *Portobello Sonnets* (Bloodaxe Books, 2017) by permission of the publisher and Rogers, Coleridge and White. Cathy Grindrod, first appeared in Candlestick poetry pamphlet. Grevel Lindop, *Tourists* (Carcanet Press, 1987). Gill McEvoy, *Uncertain Days* (Happen*Stance* Press, 2006) by kind permission of the author. Graham Mort, *Black Shiver Moss* (Seren Press, 2017). Helena Nelson, *Starlight on Water* (Rialto Press, 2003) by kind permission of the author. Kenn Nesbitt, *The Armpit of Doom* (Purple Room Publishing, 2012) © 2012 Kenn Nesbitt. All Rights Reserved. Reprinted by permission of the author. DA Prince, *Nearly the Happy Hour* (Happen*Stance* Press, 2008) by kind permission of the author.

All permissions cleared courtesy of Swift Permissions
swiftpermissions@gmail.com

Where poets are no longer living their dates are given.

Introduction

Some poets can trace their heritage back to renowned writers, and very proud they are too if they find an ancestor to be proud of. To my regret, none of my own relatives, now or in the past, was famous for writing anything. However, some of them were extremely good at baking.

At one time, my great-great-grandmother sold bread from home and sent her numerous children out to deliver it door to door. Her daughter Louisa had a modest kitchen, with only three cups and saucers – one each for herself and her husband, and a third for a visitor – but she would fill it with tray-bakes prepared for the Cricket Club tea. My grandmother, too, was a dab hand at cakes, especially meringues. She beat her egg whites by hand, using a metal plate and the blade of a knife, and my cousin can remember it.

My mother inherited the skill and aptitude. Our family never went on holiday without at least three large tins packed full of home-made cake. She was famous for flapjack and coffee cake, Simnel cake and drop scones. Later on, after a visitor from Allinson's Flour did a demonstration for the local Women's Institute, she started to make her own bread too and never looked back. When I grew up, I worked for a while in a patisserie where I mastered puff and choux pastry. After that, I was the one called in for Eccles Cakes and Mille-feuille, Danish Pastries and Apfel Strudel. And now my son and daughter, in their thirties, are continuing the cake tradition with gusto, especially at birthdays when the most extraordinary confections appear. I expect my grandchildren to follow the tradition in time – because what can be better than a house that smells of fresh baking?

It is not just a cliché that good things disappear like hot cakes. I have always thought the culinary arts are, of all artistic endeavours, the most magical. The more beautiful their creations – the finer the making – the faster they vanish. And once gone (each batch being perfectly unique) they are gone forever.

Just occasionally, however, their memories find their way into poems.

Helena Nelson

The Night Bakery

None of them are angels, all wear white,
Their light ablaze on Lennox Street, at the hour
Of breadmaking…. Where does the time go,
Anyone might ask himself, standing here
As I do, between night and morning, heaven and hell,
Breathing it in, the yeasty smell
Of everydayness, freshness for the soul
That only asks of the earth a place to dwell
In weightless ecstasy?
                              Batches cool
On the aluminium trays. No price as yet
On anything. Flies are dying, in a blue incandescence.
Somebody steps out for a cigarette.
I watch it being stirred, the mixing bowl
Of spirit and essence….

Harry Clifton

Spice Jars

They stood for years, high on the pantry shelf.
Then dust to dust: loose stoppers, grey and furred,
greasy with age, neglect, the labels blurred,
each spice surrendering its ancient self
turned pensioner-apologetic, yet
leaving a perfect circle clean when lifted
like some domestic chess piece shifted
in one last game, or stately minuet.

I opened one: faint kitchen scents (a trace
of fruit breads, Welsh cakes, and the kitchen warm
and welcoming from school) took shadow form:
allspice and nutmeg, cinnamon and mace,
caraway for seed cakes or for loaves,
and dry, black-budded rattlings of cloves.

DA Prince

Bread

It warms as I work it,
rocking heel to fingertip,
kneading it, letting it go.
The dough knits up the flour and salt,
stitching separate into whole.

I am considering
your death, my illness,
the burden of uncertain days.
I ball up tight the springy globe,
stretch it like a rubber band, let it go.

It moulds itself into a mass
of yeasty muttering,
like men straining at a heavy task,
sweats and mumbles,
making something of itself. It grows

a mushroom sponge of hope.
I punch it down. It's mine to shape.

Gill McEvoy

The Baker

I'd like to be a baker, and come when morning breaks,
Calling out, *"Beeay-ko!"* (that's the sound he makes) –
Riding in a rattle-cart that jogs and jolts and shakes,
Selling all the sweetest things a baker ever bakes;
Currant-buns and brandy-snaps, pastry all in flakes;
  But I wouldn't be a baker if…
    I couldn't eat the cakes.
      Would you?

CJ Dennis (1876 – 1938)

Mrs Philpott makes a cake

Yes – bake a cake for a visitor.
The baker is wearing a rose-bud apron.
Her hair and hands are dusted with flour.

Eggs are waiting beside the cooker.
Butter and sugar have surged to foam.
Her wooden spoon is an oval of power.

This is a cake descended of cakes
born in small ovens for generations,
a cake of fragrance and careful making.

A hint of almond is for forgiveness;
the soft lemon curd is for contrition;
vanilla hastens the shade of sweetness.

The crumb of the cake will be light and calm;
the scent of the cake will be clear as dawn,
the shape of the cake a golden sun.

It will rise, like heaven, and then be gone.

Helena Nelson

Summer Pudding
for Carole Reeves

Begin with half a pound of raspberries
picked from the deep end of your sloping garden, where the birds
        play hopscotch in the draggled fruitnets; add
a quarter of redcurrants; gently seethe in orange juice
        for six or seven minutes with some sugar,
giving the pan a ritual shake from time to time, inducing
        a marriage of those fine, compatible
tastes; and leave to cool. An open kitchen door invites
        whatever breeze will help itself to flavour,
attenuating it downhill across your neighbours' gardens
        (be generous!) so summer will surprise them,
an unidentifiable recalled fulfilment haunting
        the giant bellflower and the scarlet runners.
Now introduce your strawberries, sliced to let the pallid heartsflesh
        transfuse its juice into the mass, transmute
cooled fruit to liquid crystal while you line your bowl with bread
        and add the mixture – keeping back some juice –
lid it with bread, cover and weight it, chill it if you like
        (as if the winter took a hand) and hoard it,
opus magnum ripening its secret, edible,
        inviolable time. And when you dare
slide your knife round its socket to uncling – a sudden suck –
        this gelid Silbury mined with the wealth
of archetypal summer, let it be on one of three
        occasions: for a kitchenful of children
whose mouths grow purpleringed and flecked with whipped cream
                                                as they dig
        and lose, entranced, the treasure of the minute;
or for the friends around your polished table, when that soft
        lake of mahogany reflects the faces
melting in candlelight and burgundy, rivers of talk
        eddying to a stillness lost in taste
primitive as a language, clear as thought; or for whoever
        will join you in your garden when the sun

carries out summer to the edge of dark, and stay to eat
        there in the early chill as twilight gels
and owlhoots quiver from the gulf of darkness, where a floodlit
        cathedral floats under your eyes, and still
(wreckage of smeared plates and clotted spoons piling the table)
        after the lights are killed and the cathedral
vanishes like a switchedoff hologram, remain to plot
        the moon's progress across the brimming air
scaled by the nightscented stocks, or with binoculars
        arrest the Brownian movement of the stars.

Grevel Lindop

How to make Apple Crumble

Balance in your palm a green winter moon.

Slide a steel blade in
        to set in motion
        the fall of spiralling skin
        wheeling in rings,
        twisting its light path,
        splashing a snake-trail on marble.

Slice your naked moon.

Let flour rain
        like dust motes through sun beams
        in kitchens of glass.

Make a sweet blanket,
        rough as a cottage, pebble-dashed;
        where a witch once lived
        who stirred a spell in an earthenware dish
        the colour of sand.

Smother your slivers of apple moon
        like a fresh snowfall.

Make it white hot.

Take a cold spoon;
        dig deep to its creaking core.

Cathy Grindrod

The Toughest Pastry Maker

I'm the toughest pastry maker who has ever baked a cake.
My impressive little pastries are impossible to break.
Yes, my cookies and my cupcakes will defeat the strongest jaws,
while my muffins are impervious to power drills and saws.

You have never seen a danish or a donut quite so strong
and I bake the fiercest fruitcake that has ever come along.
You can chew on them till doomsday, you can chew till kingdom come,
but you'll never get a nibble, not a solitary crumb.

You can whack them with a hammer, you can hit them with a stick.
You can stab them with a dagger, you can beat them with a brick.
You can drop them from an airplane, you can blast them with a bomb
but my pastries will exhibit only peacefulness and calm.

I expect you'll want to test them. I encourage you to try,
but you'll never make a mark on them and here's the reason why:
I do something with my recipes no other bakers do;
when the cookbook calls for 'milk' or 'water', I use Crazy Glue.

Kenn Nesbitt

A Rising

Up at six to bake the dough that swelled with wild
spores all night, its sour dream leavening the dark.

Low sun comes with early day, cattle epic under
thorn blossom, meadow grass glassy with dew.

Shadows stretch from the roots of trees, fish ghosts
steer the gill, finning stone. Light seeps through

glass, a child snores upstairs, a toilet flushes, then
the blurred tread of footsteps. She's knocking hot

bread from the tins: its burnt rye smell, its glaze of
milk that was grass bent under rain, a Holstein's

tongue. In March, before he passed, three blackbirds
quarrelled here, cocksure duellists in tight frock

coats: now they pour this quintessence from their
throats, the purified loss of song. She sits with

a book of poems tracing the crewel-work of another
mind, its fey twist and chance. Images transpire through

space more real than this lit room, its cooling loaves.
She wonders who will come to share them first: her

boys, still sleeping with their wives? Her grandson,
his cheeks a flush of pillow-heat and apple-bloom?

Cattle raise their heads, stark and huge, staring at the
house where she is spellbound in stanzas, the hush

of rooms. Words fall out of order, rise again to make
meaning, the pages turning, faint as indrawn breath.

Graham Mort

From *Outlandish Proverbs* (1640), collected by George Herbert

Bee not a Baker if your head be of butter.
He that is at ease seeks dainties.
Hunger makes dinners, pastime suppers.

A little with quiet is the onely dyet.
A little Kitchin makes a large house.
A little and good fills the trencher.

He that hath the spice may season as he list.
All griefes with bread are lesse.
Of all smells, bread; of all tastes, salt.

Anon